# Sweetest Song I Know

Josephs Quartzy

Published by Josephs Quartzy, 2022.

SWEETEST SONG I KNOW

**First edition. November 3, 2022.**



ISBN: 979-8215697047

Written by Josephs Quartzy.

JOSEPHS QUARTZY
50+
POEMS
SWEETEST SONG I KNOW

# Acknowledgement

'Lord is always my shepherd', I surely succeed. I thank **God** before any other creature, He knows me, blesses me and keeps me alive.

I should thank myself for having me, understanding me, fighting criticism and always being strong.

Support from my wonderful fans gives me the strength to keep on writing, thinking of something new and deliver what is good.

# Author biography

**Josephs Quartzy** is a Tanzanian actor, singer and author. He is best known for playing Nhwale in the romance fiction film *Mr Local Man* and for his role in the drama series *JQ Knew That.* He is a member of the music duo, The Eastern Bandits. Josephs is the author of; A *Tale of an Intelligent Psychopath*, *Irene: The Andromeda* and *A Blessed Curse.*

# Introduction

**Sweetest song I know** is an English poetry book composed and written by **Josephs Quartzy**. This poetry book consists of more than 50 well-arranged different original poems important for mental health, relationships, places, and students, reading it will entertain, teach, remind, inform, and educate all.

This book is for all ages, ethnicities, cultures and religions for both poem lovers and anyone who never tried liking poems, "*Poetry is art, poetry is music, music heals and music gives life*", as an author, I never liked poems too, but I needed only one time of reading, a moment that changed my life forever. You are welcome to the real world of music, enjoy the best **stanzas** of the *sweetest song I know*.

# I

# STANZA FOR MENTAL HEALTH

# Don't shoot

*You take a gun, out of your pocket,*
*pointing to a man who needs to live like you,*
*shooting at him, like you are a little god,*
*taking his life, you playing grim reaper.*

*I don't understand the point of shooting,*
*I shoot you, your kids will eventually shoot me,*
*my kids will surely shoot your kids too,*
*Is that how the world was meant to be?*

*Just settle things or ignore the winds,*
*Killing is not a real deal, rather it's witchcraft,*
*we fight with money, a pen and ideas,*
*we now live in a much more civilized world, not a war zone.*

# Hero's definition

*You shut up when they want you to react,*
*you are a hero,*
*you smile when they annoy you,*
*you are a hero,*
*you believe in yourself when nobody does,*
*you are a hero,*
*you solve rather than ignore,*
*you are a hero,*
*nobody cares about you but you care,*
*you are a hero,*
*you put smiles on their faces,*
*you are a hero,*
*nobody wants you but you welcome all,*
*you are a hero,*
*you try and find than waiting,*
*you are a hero.*

## Live to live

*We saw on the news, she hanged herself,*
*we read on the paper, he chocked himself,*
*they were still young, to say enough about food,*
*age is not enough unless fate decides.*

*They were all above the hill, she threw herself,*
*They were still happy together, he shot himself,*
*saddest news, worst messages we get,*
*age is not enough unless fate decides.*

*They were still in love when they drank poison,*
*They were in a quarrel when they cut themselves,*
*what uneasiness and scarry deaths,*
*age is not enough unless fate decides.*

# Vengeance

*He killed his mother, because of anger,*
*she pushed her lover, because of anger,*
*he should have settled with her,*
*she should have hugged him instead,*

*Anger eats, anger kills,*
*jail calls, the hospital holds on-call,*
*mortuary is a life partner to anger,*
*graves are scary but not with anger.*

*Anger takes your freedom,*
*anger imprison you in jail of regrets,*
*anger takes away your friends,*
*anger makes your enemies happier.*

## We loved the way you were

*A beautiful angel you were,*
*amazing kid you were growing up to be,*
*what happened to that little kid in you,*
*that bowed when elders talked to him,*
*you talk back and make them bow instead,*
*he used to dress very smartly,*
*I saw you with torn pants going to a party,*
*he used to ask, 'can I be your friend,*
*you tell people, 'get off me, I hate noises',*
*we miss that little you, a nice kid,*
*you made them believe you take in something,*
*you loved a kid next door, now you flip to any,*
*he used to be a saint, you lie the same as your heartbeats*
*we loved the way you were.*

# Everybody loves you

*We both reach a stage of thinking wrong,*
*we underestimate ourselves, we think negatively,*
*well no, everybody loves us,*

*everybody is weak, all are strong,*
*strongest we see takes their weaknesses as strengths,*
*you should remember, everybody loves you,*

*you're black, he's white, what's the problem,*
*I'm short, you're tall, I believe I'm fine,*
*the problem will come if I think I'm not enough,*

*I'm crippled, you're fine, we both live,*
*you drive, I walk, and we both inhale oxygen,*
*don't think too hard, everybody loves you.*

## Well, we knew you were a rapper

*Trillion tattoos, a ton of metals hanging on your neck,*
*shaggy clothes, torn pants and so-called swagger,*
*will that make you a good rapper?*
*Well, we knew you were a rapper.*

*Using explication and harsh words,*
*insulting anybody, elders even leaders,*
*will that make you a good rapper?*
*Well, we knew you were a rapper.*

*A rapper is defined by music, not lifestyle,*
*rhythm and punch lines will surely define you,*
*and that will make you a good rapper,*
*well, we will know you are the best rapper.*

## Say 'NO'

*I give you drugs to try, say no,*
*you don't drink, I'm trying to convince you to, say no,*
*you don't smoke I give you a piece, say no,*
*you don't a club, you are happy when I try to speak, say no*
*you are reading, I stop you, say no,*
*I promise to marry you but it's a lie, say no,*
*you know you are great, If I troll you, say no,*
*if I tell you I'm better than you, say no,*
*they underestimate your capabilities, tell them no.*

# I'm colored too

*Do you believe coloured skin is a sin? Well, I don't,*
*nobody cares about colours anymore,*
*anything trolling colour should try being a human first,*
*If they use your colour to say you're weak,*
*crying means you accept your colour is bad,*
*protesting means, you accept what they say but you don't want to hear it,*
*trying to change it means you don't like it too,*
*ignoring is bad but worth trying,*
*every colour is strong as well as very weak,*
*beauty is created by eyes, not with theories,*
*don't think too much when you are trolled,*
*because we never give a chance to negativity,*
*just think you are strong, and you will realize those strengths.*

## Why killing?

*We know in this world of God, satan lives too,*
*he collects his people, killers as his generals,*
*God created somebody, Mr nobody destroys,*
*God gives life, somebody's child takes it.*

*They live to think they can be gods,*
*they challenge God as their nephew,*
*they act brutal and too crazy to worry about the consequences,*
*they don't realize that they are alive they should not kill,*

*If they ever think they need a challenger,*
*we present death itself before them*
*let the challenge begin,*
*you can't create why killing,*
*you didn't plant, why harvesting,*
*you are not a god, stop killing*

## Generational trauma

*Dad said don't rap or you will smoke weed,*
*mama said don't stand before a camera or be an addict,*
*grandpa said I must become a doctor,*
*grandma said I was meant to be a lawyer.*

*My Aunt reported when I joined a street band,*
*uncle canned me whenever I bought headphones,*
*you won't have to dance or you will break your bones,*
*don't go swimming, that's not the real man's job.*

*cooking is for shes not for a big man,*
*don't wash, what's your wife for?*
*I disagree because,*
*we can't change the game, but rules can be adjusted,*
*we will be late if generational trauma still feeds in us.*

# A better world

*What if the world is poison free?*
*What if the world is hate free?*
*What if the world is killing free?*
*only we can make it a better place.*

*What if the world is full of love?*
*What if the world is full of happiness?*
*no racism, mass shootings or cries?*
*only we can make it a better place.*

*A better world was made by God,*
*given to us to maintain what was made,*
*It was shaped differently by only us,*
*only we can make it a better place.*

# Do you read?

*reading gives knowledge, gives wings,*
*gives imagination, gives dreams,*
*reading ideas improves,*
*reading stories entertains,*
*reading the news informs,*
*reading books teaches,*
*reading the song rhymes.*
*I said 'a' and learned to draw it,*
*I write because I read how to write,*
*do you read?*

# Escape

*Escape from your weaknesses,*
*escape from fake friends,*
*escape from a goalless company,*
*escape from identified troubles,*
*escape from what doesn't matter,*
*escape from what's never necessary,*
*escape from bad hype,*
*escape from doing drugs,*
*escape from excessive alcoholism,*
*escape from unsafe sex,*
*escape from peer groups,*
*all you have to do is escape from negativity.*

## Don't cry anymore

*The world has never been unfair, we all suffer,*
*Love is always unfair, we both felt the same,*
*Life is never fair, we both experience,*
*we are on a test, don't cry anymore.*

*Poverty is everywhere around us,*
*even governments encounter big debts,*
*fights were ever here before our ancestors,*
*we found everything, don't cry anymore.*

*The tongue tastes sweet, sour and bitter,*
*It doesn't perish because it lives to taste both,*
*you are human after all, leaving means a lot*
*life is better lived, don't cry anymore.*

*always hope for the best, dream the best*
*even though the worst awaits as our challenger,*
*dying is the only end of the road,*
*don't give up, don't cry anymore.*

## II

## STANZA OF LOVE

## No one loves you as I do

*When I first saw you, in a corner shop,*
*when my heart suddenly out it popped,*
*I regret passing, I should have stopped,*
*because when he hold you, I felt robbed,*

*The day you smiled at me in that bar,*
*the moment my heart and brain started the war,*
*I thought maybe I'm not the right guy,*
*but I know, no one loves you as I do.*

*Just yesterday you said, yes I do,*
*If I give my life will that still do?*
*I made names for you, baby and boo,*
*you should know, no one loves you as I do*

# Kiss from a princess

*A kiss from a princess, a princess of Narnia,*
*a kiss from a princess, a princess of fairies,*
*her kiss gives me life, takes away my sorrows,*
*she is close, his scent exceeds that of Jasmine,*
*her warmth melts all the ice in me,*
*whatever happens after, I tend to forget them all,*
*because she lets me in her world of no memory,*
*a world of a kiss from a princess.*

# All I know

*Love me all I know,*
*I would say*
*If I get the time to show my love to you,*
*that my heart's for you*
*remains here today*
*forever we gonna stay and start here t0day".*

*As I know,*
*that you're gone*
*as if you are here with me forever*
*I'll hug you,*
*I gonna keep you*
*Hey come back here and dance here today*

## sometimes

*Sometimes, we conquer the world through our minds,*
*sometimes we love but also we feel the pain,*
*sometimes I dream only about your love,*
*sometimes I hear only about my songs*

## My life

*My life has been easy-too nice, these days I'm in love, I swear, born new,*
*Took my life, my heart, my love, my feelings,*
*you see, It's you, You're there*

*This is real, I swear, never lied, no more tears*
*When hard, I cried and never tried, but I'm going to,*
*when first i saw you,*
*it's my heart stopped for a while never knew what It gonna do,*
*You're the one this I'm writing to,*
*just smile and laugh,*
*whenever out, before I get in through,*
*you're always, my mamasita, senorita, snow-winter*
*be alive*

*What I think, what I guess Love won't be too easy,*
*so,*
*don't rush, no more tears, I beg,*
*at least,*
*Worry out, don't rush, don't cry,*
*You're in love I know, hang on, I'll be there.*

## In a few words

*In a few words, I love you,*
*and I'll say that, I need you,*
*In my heart, I'll write to you,*
*I'll cherish your precious big love.*

*I'm a knight of your perfect love,*
*You cool eyes, your whole you,*
*I'm a fighter for your love,*
*your day, your hubby and shield.*

*In my world, I welcome you,*
*you're welcome, welcome to me,*
*in my heart, you're my pillars,*
*you are my mom, sister and wife.*

# Forever will

*forever we said,*
*together we will stay,*
*no matter how hard it becomes,*
*together will is me and you.*

*seeing the light, feeling the night,*
*doing right, throwing all wrongs,*
*touching or pushing, sitting or walking far,*
*far beyond pal.*

*I don't believe, we walked like that,*
*I can't imagine, we have the point,,*
*If we go on like this, we'll reach far,*
*in clouds, shooting like stars.*

*in the night we'll shine,*
*with the light, we'll grow,*
*in the dark, we're lit, like candles on the wall,*
*will shoot like arrows.*

*Forever will surely bring forth,*
*like the sun went only for a night,*
*in the morning there it comes to light,*
*at that time we pray we'll never be lost.*

*forever is not seen or reached,*
*it's obtained through feelings,*
*piercing through times in the heart,*
*to see me and you in forever will.*

# Trenches

*I've run to the west and east,*
*I've looked into woods and waters,*
*I've climbed all hills and heights,*
*but I found you and your love.*

*I went down to sea shore,*
*I searched seas and all the trenches,*
*I've gone beyond normal reaches,*
*left none of the mountains to climb higher.*

*Your love is what I found there,*
*no matter what I search,*
*you're mine to find,*
*Always I find you and you're loved.*

*you were there between the alley,*
*waiting for me in the bushes,*
*In the woods, you waited, like a log stature,*
*In the rain, you waited no matter how you were washed.*

*you found me as I found you,*
*you called me when I went ahead with the post,*
*waved at me, when you saw me coming,*
*what about a hug you gave me when I was close?*

*we were in lookouts, looking for us,*
*the world shaded us, distracted from us too,*
*looking was our priority, looking was our goal,*
*we gladly found us, we made us proud.*

# Evergreen

*I got a flower, green it is,*
*I found a tower, it's evergreen,*
*I found a power that's all green,*
*I found a girl who loves greens,*
*what should you can me, a love of greens,*
*she wears her clothes, full of greens,*
*she found me too, a lover of greens,*
*she makes a garden, that is evergreen,*
*what should I call her a love of greens,*
*We'll marry too sweet, on lands of greens,*
*we'll get the kids, that love greens,*
*will make a garden, that's evergreen,*
*what should they call us, a family of greens?*

# III

## JOSEPHS QUARTZY

## SADDEST STANZA

# Death

*If I was told to say about the saddest moments,*
*death is the topic,*
*If I was told to opt-out of the worst stage in life,*
*death is the choice,*
*If I was told to curse the most disgusting thing,*
*death I would cursed,*
*death is a stage of going somewhere and nowhere,*
*going where nobody knows where is where,*
*If choices to hate come in,*
*death I must hate, because,*
*If we are told to live forever,*
*death would say no,*
*If we wish to stay with our loved ones,*
*death chooses to take them.*

## Missing anthem

*I used to troll her, I said, she was never good enough,*
*She cried, she begged but my mind never felt her,*
*tears streamed down her eyes the day she left me,*
*she said, least you are happy and I can now smile.*

*I wouldn't understand because I was busy with me,*
*I thought she will never live without me, but I'm wrong,*
*All alone on my bed, her pillow is what I watch the most,*
*I don't have an appetite for anything, I hate everything.*

*"leave me alone", I recall when she comes into my mind*
*I told her without hesitation, without fearing myself,*
*I now think of punishing myself, but how can I?*
*Her hating me is the whole world against me.*

*I see her in my sleep, I can't work coz she's looking at me,*
*I feel guilty about anything I touch, anything I'm running to,*
*She's now engaged, I know and I miss her more,*
*this curse of lonely I cursed myself will never let me off.*

# Forgive me

*Should I call you dear or love?*
*Can you hear me or not?*
*I know I'm wrong, you're not,*
*I made a mistake, a bad turn,*
*hear me out, help me up,*
*your forgiveness is my strength,*
*moving forward is impossible,*
*If you don't allow me to,*
*I want to realize the power of forgiveness,*
*please let me experience its beauty,*
*let my heart warm up when you raise me,*
*when you hug me tight, close to your forgiving heart.*

# IV

## STANZA OF JOY

# The winds of change

*winds of change were choices I made,*
*wonders to take, I didn't play a chase,*
*whatever I chose, very thoughtful I was,*
*whatever you do, be the wind of change.*

*days went on so fast, time passed by,*
*but tomorrow, time still counted on,*
*the same numbers, the same style,*
*whatever you do, be the wind of change.*

*My parents shouted, elders cursed,*
*choices I made, made fun of me,*
*I was seen as a looser, but I turned into a winner,*
*whatever you do, be the wind of change.*

*society corrects, but also suggests,*
*you are made by you, not any other pests,*
*considering others' ideas, you only make choices,*
*whatever you do, be the wind of change.*

# What a wonderful world

*Have you seen butterflies flying across the gardens?*
*have you seen deer completing the beauty of the greens?*
*what about fish swimming fast in water?*
*ooh what a wonderful world we live in.*

*I once saw birds in the sky and felt for the world,*
*I visited the pond to hear frogs sing with the voices of joy,*
*goosebumps greeted me when I saw peacock rattling,*
*ooh what a wonderful world we live in.*

*trees sing when the wind visit, glasses dance when the tree sings,*
*wonderful wonderful wind your visit brings us happiness,*
*in gardens, forests, backyards or inside houses they're hot,*
*ooh what a wonderful world we live in.*

*Cold comes to bless us with that feeling.*
*warmth comes each year to warm us and prepare us,*
*rains are blessings we receive because water is life,*
*ooh what a wonderful world we live in.*

*lands of all types including clay, sand, soil and many more,*
*they bless not only humans but plants, insects even life,*
*it gives us life, food and shelter to live in,*
*ooh what a wonderful world to live in.*

*we are humans, we rule the lands no matter how we look,*
*fair or coloured, we make garden earth very beautiful,*
*after all, we are the flowers to nourish the world,*
*ooh, what a wonderful world we live in.*

# V

# SELF STANZA

# Silence

*silence solves problems, reduces fights,*
*silence makes you wise, among the noisemakers,*
*silence teaches surrendering, teaches surprising,*
*silence reduces enemies, reduces garbage.*

*silence serves time, for you and yourself,*
*though it tells nothing, it gives everything,*
*silence promotes individuality, gives wings to fly,*
*silence is limitless, silence makes you concentrate.*

# Jack of all trades

*I'm Jack, yes Jack of all trades,*
*I walk every way, I win every game,*
*my goal with my breath,*
*to get whatever is on the way,*
*because I'm Jack, a Jack of all trades.*

*I hit their roads, they hate me a lot,*
*I care less about what they say, or what they do,*
*All I do, I do for me, I do my ways,*
*because I'm Jack, a Jack of all trades.*

*If they hold me back, I'll hold their necks,*
*they tend to spoil, I'll cut those craps,*
*All I do is to win, win every game I'm in,*
*because I'm Jack, a Jack of all trades.*

# Goals

*Without a goal, there's no direction,*
*without a focus, there's no point,*
*we are born to live, living to survive,*
*I have a goal, you better look for yours.*

*Want to own a big launch, that's my goal,*
*Plans to own a big house, that's his goal,*
*fighting to be a lawyer, that's her goal,*
*we have goals, you better look for yours.*

*goals make us know where we stand,*
*goals give meaning to timekeeping,*
*goals award us life improvements,*
*they have goals, you better look for yours.*

*without a goal, you'll live like an animal,*
*no one ever seeks advice from a donkey or hyena,*
*he will never know where to go because goalless blinds,*
*If we both have goals, you better look for yours.*

# I don't care

*Why should you hate me?*
*Why should you want to fight me?*
*Was I ever bad to you?*
*Did I ever offend you?*
*Is my presence a nuisance?*
*Is my well-being a mistake?*
*Was my birth a mistake?*
*If none of the reasons matters*
*why do you hate for no reason at all?*
*Even though I hate being hated,*
*I never hate because I was hated first,*
*I don't care at all*

# VI

# HYPE STANZA

## Wanna dance?

*If you care wanna dance, then dagg more,*
*wanna bang if you like then have more,*
*Long time, more time that nobody knows,*
*Born town, yes, but no money then no swag talks,*
*Big mind don't mind let her be mine,*
*snitches dare wanna burn then lit high,*
*Come on baby girl ain't a bad guy,*
*Yo love I surrender you're my only one.*

# Look how I do

*look how I do it, look how I dance,*
*look how I jump higher above,*
*look how I'm bold not how I'm old,*
*look how I get what's higher above,*
*I think I'm clear, about what I do,*
*I guess I'm done, for what it's done,*

## Birthdays

*we are born to live, live to rise,*
*rise to walk, walk and run,*
*running to your day,*
*to wish you abundant life,*
*happy life, good life,*
*a successful life, of course, longer life.*

# VII

## STANZA OF COMFORT

# Sometimes

*There you are here I am in a game,*
*a game that we must come and play,*
*And find a way, to pass through that gate,*
*Sometimes we plant, sometimes we plan,*
*sometimes we rise higher more n more to shine,*
*sometimes we love, and of course, we hate,*
*sometimes we hug, sometimes we quarrel,*
*sometimes those are times to live for.*

## It's all in you

*It takes a few days to complete cycling the world,*
*but it takes forever to understand its ways,*
*whatever, you need none of all that in you,*
*but you need to live in it.*

*every push and pull there must be force applied,*
*physics reminds us to always get it that way,*
*It's true, nothing changes without sacrifice,*
*that reminds you, you need to live in it.*

# Come on

*come on, move on,*
*we can reach tomorrow,*
*pull on, keep going,*
*it's all in your strength,*
*come up, go on,*
*we can see the shore,*
*reach up, dig up,*
*let's make it tomorrow.*

# VIII

## STANZA OF PRAISES

# Nights

*Through the nights, piercing seconds,*
*none stays awake, none bluffs a sentence,*
*nobody stands, sometimes until morning,*
*time to rest, until morning lights.*

*frogs sing rats dance,*
*night bell rings, bat wrap their wings,*
*eyes close, our bodies grow,*
*a better night's sleep saves a brighter day.*

*nights take our sorrows,*
*good nights bring our tomorrows,*
*big darkness reminds us of horror,*
*with a night, we work all day long.*

## A house, a wonderful friend

*Birds in their house of grasses, make a family,*
*they enjoy a home, they live their dreams,*
*we talk about a house, we talk about a friend,*
*a protector, who takes all outside dangers for us,*
*heat, rain, sun rays, terrorism even excessive cold,*
*a house gives us a place to make and have a family,*
*oh dear house, what a wonderful friend,*
*sometimes you witness our birth, you cheer,*
*you even live to witness our deaths, you cry,*
*you give people dreams, you give them ambitions,*
*we go on because you allow us to use you,*
*what a great company we have in this world.*

## A beautiful day

*What a morning, what a day,*
*what a scent, this is today,*
*what a beautiful, start to the day*
*I'll be walking, going all ways.*

*I'll be moving, towards evening light,*
*I'll follow it, until the night,*
*I won't sleep until midnight,*
*I have to finish this wonderful day.*

# Music everywhere

*Frogs sing,*
*birds rhyme,*
*animals sound,*
*trees dance,*
*humans vocalize,*
*winds whistle,*
*music is everywhere,*
*songs are anywhere,*
*all creatures make a song,*
*the sweetest song I Know.*

# Kilimanjaro

*Ooh, the tallest peak in Africa,*
*your prestige proceeds any of the peaks in the world,*
*I saw you once, and only one time I felt for you,*
*Your beauty makes a complete meaning of beauty,*
*all around the world, people want to come and see you,*
*hug your smooth soil and hold your sweet rocks,*
*your two heads wear white beautiful ice coats,*
*we call them Kibo and Mawenzi, ooh beauty peaks,*
*the name Kilimanjaro will always go down in history,*
*you always remind us to be proud because you are here,*
*you give us beauty, money, employment and all,*
*ooh, the tallest peak in Africa.*

## Zanzibar

*As a kid, I loved to visit a place everyone wants to go,*
*where colours, tribes, cultures, nations and religions go,*
*Zanzibar, a place of wonders in wonderland,*
*a right place my mind illustrated for me when I slept,*
*surrounded by waters of beauty and a breath of life,*
*with well-cultured, good looking and kindest people,*
*I found a place in my heart, Zanzibar is my dream.*

*Holy scriptures identify Caanan, well I see Zanzibar,*
*my caanan, everybody's Caanan a wonder Caanan,*
*Swahili, baghrashia, fish, coconuts, mtori, these are real,*
*beaches, music, scenery, and whatever you can dream of,*
*palm trees along the roads, beautiful and cultured ladies,*
*mighty, nice, and kindest gentlemen are of Zanzibar,*
*I found a place in my heart, Zanzibar is my dream.*

*Forodhani is not a fairy tale from a tale book,*
*but a real place in my Caanan, a place of joy,*
*waters, foods, music, culture, buildings, that's a place,*
*whenever I visited a place, I thought I would never leave,*
*I must miss it more and more to ever dream of it more,*
*I don't describe a place in heaven, it is on earth, here,*
*I found a place in my heart, Zanzibar is my dream.*

## Serengeti

*God gave me what everyone ever wanted,*
*to be born near any of the seven wonders of the world,*
*I'm talking about the famous and beautiful Serengeti,*
*difficult to explain in a poem or elaborate in a book.*

# Rain

*Let it rain? let waterfall,*
*rain gives life because water is life,*
*rain cools me when I'm hot,*
*when the world is dry, rai is missed,*
*some say god is crying so that we celebrate,*
*his tears fill the earth with joy,*
*where you rain, relieve our pain.*

## Adventurer

*In China, he saw the Himalayas and a great wall,*
*In the US she saw a statue of liberty and multiculturalism,*
*In Dubai, they saw the amazing Burj Khalifa,*
*In Russia, we experienced very cool weather,*
*Switzerland with beautiful scenery and the biggest bank,*
*He can't forget the tallest tower in France,*
*beautiful culture maintenance in Japan,*
*we witnessed the kindest people in India,*
*Kilimanjaro and Serengeti, I'm talking about Tanzania,*
*Pyramids with the Nile the great complete Egypt,*
*What beautiful beaches of Australia,*
*An enjoyable fine world in Brazil,*
*Have you ever tasted Italian dishes, well they did,*
*I saw beautiful people in Korea too,*
*Let's be adventurers, let's explore the world.*

# IX

## FAMILY STANZA

# Our last born

*He annoyed, he annoyed me,*
*especially when he cried for my things,*
*you better surrender than wait for his noise,*
*they cared for him so much to make me feel sad,*
*Am I a child too, or kind of adopted?*
*All in all, I knew, he was our last born.*

*How crazy I was, to envy my brother,*
*because I forgot I was upgraded into a big brother,*
*soon or later, I would be his big coach,*
*I better love him because now is the only time we have,*
*all in all, I knew he was our last born.*

*He is now a grown-up, not a little boy anymore,*
*oh, we have another young, I mean the last born,*
*his turn is heartwarming,*
*because I feel like every debt is paid,*
*all in all, he knows, she is our last born.*

## Father's time

*Time to be with me, you filled me up,*
*and,*
*when I said you are bad, you brought me bread,*
*I remember,*
*Times I thought you are a torturer, you were hurt for me,*
*in fact,*
*your curses at me, all built my life beautifully,*
*as a grown-up,*
*yelling throughout the nights, I now know why,*
*at times,*
*I thought you are a bully, but I was wrong,*
*because*
*you saw what was coming, I saw what was there,*
*to me,*
*all I saw was an obstacle, in my loved life ways,*
*but,*
*you were my invisible shield, from life's bad wills,*
*I now know,*
*you came earlier, to teach me well,*
*to be honest,*
*I'm glad I found a hero in my father.*

# Mother's

*never lived with my mom,*
*to say how their love would be,*
*but I've seen enough to sing,*
*their love is unmeasurable,*
*their love is incomparable,*
*piercing through time,*
*I saw how birds hold their young,*
*lioness playing with her cubs,*
*a goat feeding her kids,*
*humans hugging their children,*
*taking knives for their children,*
*cry whenever their kids fall,*
*I wished I could be among the little ones,*
*you are the best lovers ever.*

## Family comes first

*Thickest in the blood is not about relationships only,*
*family is far more than spilt blood itself,*
*family is bigger than the whole world,*
*whatever you think, family comes first.*

*any family has members, everyone is a member,*
*family needs its members, family needs everyone,*
*without a family, you are a stray being,*
*whatever you are, family comes first.*

*You travel north, remember south is where your family is,*
*family always make a welcoming home for you,*
*if the world turns against me, to my family I'll run,*
*whenever you go, family comes first.*

*Decisiveness you get, leaving your family behind,*
*kills both you and the blood inside your body,*
*Because a nightmare is when a family turns against you,*
*You have to know, family always comes first.*

*Tales of parents leaving their children alone,*
*stories of kids abandoning their old parents,*
*blood relatives or close friends fight each other,*
*I'm pretty sure none of them knows, family comes first.*

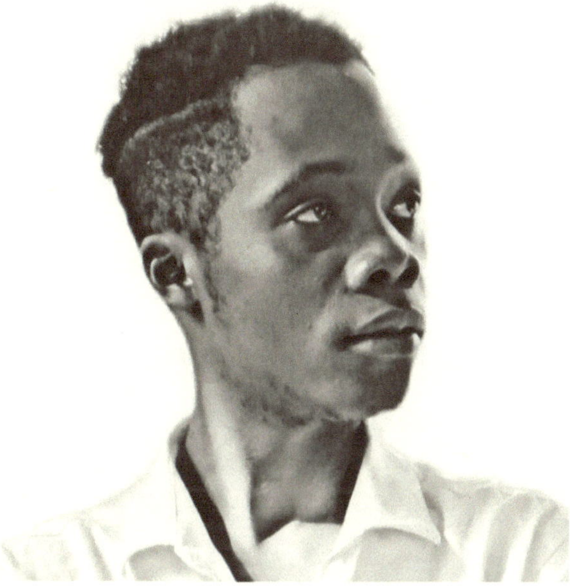

## About the Author

Josephs Quartzy is a Tanzanian actor, singer, podcaster and author. He is best known for playing Nhwale in the romance fiction film Mr Local Man and for his role in the drama series JQ Knew That. He is a member of the music duo, The Eastern Bandits. Josephs is the author of; A Taleof an Intelligent Psychopath, Irene: The Andromeda and many more.

www.ingramcontent.com/pod-product-compliance
Lightning Source LLC
LaVergne TN
LVHW090331210926
848480LV00004B/1373